dissolve

dissolve

poems by Holaday Mason

First Edition
Library of Congress Control Number: 2010935143
ISBN: 978-0-89823-259-2
American Poetry Series
Author photo ©akarnophotography.com
Cover and interior design by Katie Hamness

The publication of *Dissolve* is made possible by the generous support of the McKnight
Foundation and other contributors to New Rivers Press.

For academic permission or copyright clearance please contact Frederick T. Courtright
at 570-839-7477 or permdude@eclipse.net.

New Rivers Press is a nonprofit literary press associated with
Minnesota State University Moorhead.

Alan Davis, Senior Editor
Suzanne Kelley, Managing Editor
Wayne Gudmundson, Consultant
Allen Sheets, Art Director
Thom Tammaro, Poetry Editor
Kevin Carollo, MVP Poetry Coordinator
Fran Zimmerman, Business Manager

Publishing Interns:
Ryan Christiansen, Katelin Hansen, Jenny Hilleren, Samantha Jones, Tarver Mathison,
Jenna Miller, Elizabeth Zirbel

Dissolve Book Team: Brianna Brickweg, John Enger, Adam Heidebrink, Dan Nygard

Printed in the United States of America

New Rivers Press
c/o MSUM
1104 7th Avenue South
Moorhead, MN 56563
www.newriverspress.com

For Dr. Erna

Mort

— *The note sounded on a hunting horn to announce the death of a deer.*

Contents

One

Moth

Will I open the door? Yes,
　　　I'll release you.

　　　⤿

You've been here all night,
　　　soft as dust.

　　　⤿

Now we both know too well
　　　an impenetrable nature.

　　　⤿

What was it that *you* whispered
　　　into the panic — ?

Stained

How love, you pushed
adamantly the quiet day —

like one white feather to soil,
the planes to Paris
as estranged as your familiar touch.

We don't escape
the address of god —

small lions everywhere
in the architecture of light.

And serious thought comes
to capture us with so much
halting collapse.
            Now you

and the questions are wed
like muscle to bone.

We could

talk ad-nauseum into
            the circle of two
(your piano, my surname, the marks),

but the limits of language
fill the sky. The whole

borrowed sky.

Quandary

He is gone
insanely into winter,

though he loved her once beyond himself,
       which is, as he states, The Problem.

Remember him, love? That one young buck
       snow blind in the frozen trees,
       how we stopped the car, stopped
       breathing in —
everything swollen with new ice on old leaves.

Starting again is impossible —
also unavoidable.

His solution began at the start of August.
And it seemed it would never cease. How
       she'd stopped breathing in.

How he came undone inside her
as she unraveled,
as he careened north
to his past and his future, spurred
into hard, unimaginable winter.

       Not wise, she thinks but cannot find
her breastbone, her white pubis.

Not wise, or was it that he never
had a face and she was
just a whistle in the dark?

Dream, Somewhere in September

I hear a baby crying. The sea is crawling
into me, coming up wild again
as if I could find him in this empty world . . .
He called from St. Louis, near the twisting

Mississippi. He called from the Petrified
Forest, then for his mother, in his sleep.
He hasn't called and won't again — no need
really, he's reached the trees.

Hear that crying child again, you hear?
It's wailing really, while planes overhead fly
somewhere else, easily, and out of the blue,

I remember that old horse in the grain field
after he finally stopped begging at the barb wire
fence for food. How I slept out in that meadow,

the high dry grass coiled with rattlesnakes
and coral bells, in early April,
under the quilt of morphine moonlight,

in my beautiful youthful ivory limbs,
before final Farewell to Spring released
singed, yet still pearled sheer pink petals
over the sweltering yellowing land.

Now count these ten steps to the bed.
Brush my hair two hundred strokes

then add ten more. Now breaks my
first morning alone in nineteen years.

It doesn't have to make sense
how the mind works. Why should it?
Nothing else does.

Flight

In the seat next to me
your absence is a presence —

the new companion that follows.

Crushed shell desert below
        and each solo

cloud a paradox — shadows
like huge children.

The womb lifts only once

to let you out into this world.

Far below, irregular

rivulets of water carve the soil,

the green of human planting, arbitrary
as leaves curling up

a dead-end alley. I crossed

the desert, then the cold sea
spilled behind.

You were the only you for me,
before imagined fate

or affinity. Outside, the gathering
of clouds into a black mass

and the strangeness of strangers.

Today, death is not what I fear.

Familiar Spring Scenery, Using a Broad Brush

Years ago,
after an affair
with a woman named Susan,
you coaxed me,
like a remorseful boy,
to the mossy shade
of your childhood woods —
a place where, at the right time
of year, Lilies of the Valley
drive angelic bells
up through dense soil
after the last
of the thaw.

I wore peach
and pink cotton.
Your mother exclaimed
from her kitchen
on my good choice
of hues, nervous,
not understanding,
I suppose, our violent
fights as they drilled
through those East Coast nights,
where, in our dark history
(you know, I know) we
were wandering around
alone.

But I still longed for you,
so taped the torn
wedding vows,
lay like a swan
in the pine damp dark
and took you
back in, because I knew
this might heal

the bruising of love
gone here and there
in its truth, its deceit,
in its wandering.

Now, after
eighteen years,
your father means
to sell that piece of land,
funds for better living,
paying drug costs
without crossing the border
into Canada. We go
where we must
to get what we have to —
you know that, baby,
as you persuade
the sound of snowfall
from a borrowed upright's
black and white keys,
while the rightful owner
swims in Belize,
her too-young ex-husband
bashing into bar fights,
yanking dandelions
from their old bungalow's lawn,
not knowing that it's
really, finally, over.

At night I still love
to drive fast with
the windows rolled down,
the dusty heater beating
back cold like a fist.
It always seems to be winter
when lovers leave.
But you and me, we

still have good arms,
they still work
pretty well. I mean,
look in the garden,
thrusting spears springing up.
Yellow iris in sheer
golden torsos like gods.
I didn't plant them,
yet they appeared
long ago in a poem
where I arranged
bulbs to bloom
in concentric circles,
like fires within fires
and now look at them
out there, my love —
my love.
I don't say that enough
do I — *my love?*

San Miguel

There is a sudden downpour
and people cluster waiting
in the cove of the cathedral.
Under each arc of eve —
rain black doves.
"It is very beautiful."
"Yes, yes,"
a strange man agrees twice.
Orange lilies lie wilting
in the heat. Candles
of torn sunlight slip over us.
I have a fever and need ice.
The beggars for alms
hold out palms full of rain.
And the thunder, and
then counting the fierce
voices in the sky.
What can I bring
to bring you these stained bells,
the scent of creosote and chili,
each bent back of each woman
across the square weaving
baskets, selling sliced cactus
and pale pink carnations?
Three days I've had no bath,
should step out in the water
and be cleaned.
And I can't believe
you aren't with me —
a lost color,
a breathless lung.
People leave
the shelters of doorways
for rough cobblestone streets,
everyone watching the sky,
and when the shower has passed
an old man exits the chapel,
arms laden with huge lilies —
white and fragrant,
fragrant, white.

Outside the Church of the Freedom Fighters

Ten *pesos* for pomegranate seeds
and *churros* I eat in the last shady spot
on the square near the bus stop.
Four days I've left prayers in the church
under the gaze of a pink confection–spun
Madonna who looks directly into
my sick heart. Here you can use a word
like heart, you must because it's truth.

My sad heart, my open heart
over which I beg the Holy Ghost
to throw any old *rebozo,* shawl
for carrying the newborn, what is
precious, myself and you, *mi esposo* too.

In the market, I shoot two photos
of Indians who hate my crude theft
of their image, which I understand,
but do so I can carry them
home to the you
of my constant address,
your *corazon,* my own
and the blessed Trinity
of the *gringo* god.

I give one small girl
two pesos, almost nothing,
and another my nearly full cup
of red seeds, red tears.
I tell her mother I'm not sick —
no enferma, no illness of the body.
So she lets her child take
the sweet fruit from me.

Quiet. Blue. Murder.

He is weeping in the other room.
She goes to him though
it's over already. Her body:
a white frozen lake
crackling with ice.
His chest might break. So
she sits awake in the chair
near the bed because
it's inhumane not to. Wants
to say, "Your leaving me
won't keep death away,"
but doesn't because it would
just make him angry, that special
mean hound at her heels
she no longer wants near.
So she reminds him instead about
the old hippie breathing technique
that helps one sleep, helps staunch
night terrors. Breathe in. Count
to eight. Breathe out.
Repeat until you
forget to.

Dream of the Blue Woman

That night I dream of you with another woman and I kill her.
This proves futile since she is dead already. Still, I slit her throat,
then sew her neck back to her head because I forgot to ask her
why she's named herself after me and why she's turned so blue.

Never a Religious Man,

he set a Gideon's
on his bedside table

as if the black
pebbled leather cover
might shed light
on his path,

constructed from something
he couldn't understand
but *had to do.*

He was unhappy
with the text —
railed
at the different versions
of language, of
interpretation.

I can stand no music.
I can stand no music
or words with music,
but especially no music —

blood, whore,
candle, shoot, cunt,
contralto, Oleander,
skeletal,
slow, slow —

no, no Brahms,
especially no Bach.

Two

Patterns of Migration

At the piano again, the man makes up songs
of lost shoes, staying too late and drinking more
under the unhinged neon of some bar where
inside the big mirror he's just one more tiny drinker.

And the long compositions shift
into shadows nearly as forgotten as a snow-flurry
where once he wrote my name eight or nine times
(in long hand) in the condensation on the living

room windows, as if outlining a crime scene,
or searching for the perimeter of my body
in the letters — when it's always been smell that draws
desire, as each morning, his mother's huge dog

followed me uninvited up and down
the icy birch–lined road. In each standard
suburban house, bodies lie still, toss or rummage
around, faces form in tree bark and cars,

and we're the people across the street
from the people across the street and he
is just another man of scars caught in the odd
orbit of this particular night. Sleepless, I watch

birds fly in formation going, god only knows,
the wrong way at this time of year. And last night
I said exactly who I wanted to fuck, other than him,
because there's little meaning to be made of anything

but the rapid moves of the human eye searching
for light, seeking recognition, the retrieval over
and again of what's familiar, the way he plays it alive —
the way a woman brushes back her white hair with one hand.

Morning

But he had already done it.
Now her eyes remove him
as the sun throws soiled bars
across the bedroom where
both hearts are caged,
forgiveness/bitterness —
two flawed coals.

Two Bars, One Right after the Other

1.
See me? There I am, near the flamenco guitarist,
veiled in sheer curtains of smoke. Yes, men still stare,
but tell not one new story. I had a lover once
give me ten more years of real beauty —
that was twenty years ago. The night is lit
with paper stars in the trees and I confuse them
with the bright eyes of wild beasts —
the wishes of children. Looking at me,
the guitarist plays beautifully over the heads
of tourists in from Mexico City, slick women
with kohl–dark eyes, gold jewelry, more crosses than stars.
Tomorrow you'll fly to the Cape to bury your friend
near the sea. May you take your hate for me
in your best tweed coat, may it come back bittersweet,
trembling like the poor bee drowning in my margarita.
Festivals are meant as celebrations of hope, passage
or release, and there are none this month.
But the men down here adore my freckled shoulders —
a Mexican opera to soothe the sadness of a departed
husband. If you taste someone else I'll never know,
and vice–versa. The guitarist stops to smoke, his eyes
lingering long on my skin, and I wonder
if he ever really gets to play down the moon,
play like an unpaid whore,
until that same sliver you'll be under *mañana*
drops out of the eastern sky. *Triste esposo, con cuidado,*
danger is leaning in every doorway selling cheap cigarettes.

2.
He writes the word for yellow on a napkin — *amarillo* —
sunlight and gold dust. Alone in bars, people talk freely
to unknown people — of the lost family sugar mill,
of crazy wives and surfing mythic waves off Kilauea,

the size of any great love. Happy hour, they call it,
drinking away the high altitude of loneliness.
The waiter insists on two margaritas, though I insist
on drinking just one. Something good must come
from this stupor and heat and I won't think
of your scent — that would be like a watery
slope where whatever happens, you don't look down,
but tuck up and roll, roll, roll, roll.

Eclipse

Then I am begging,

sliding simply into

animal, animal uncoiled

in flames,

repeated as animal, repeated.

And what half–dark thing wouldn't want this —

to be pulled into

the pure root of white heat?

And what is the sound
of the lost self, rising

into the mouth of another?

Lathe. Slow. Humming. Breath.

It was such wide low tide.

And it was his moon lost to the darkness.

What you spoke of were stars

and lakes reflecting stars

and though I know too well illusion,

I wanted to be swallowed and uncovered, to descend —

then just to drown.

Dream, Untitled

I am not a woman men love,
but a woman sleep loves.
One who bit bold bracelets
        around each wrist in
the annual rage of April, of those born
        who protest being born. I am
the woman who chanted tarantulas
from under parched cactus
while her lovers kissed
        her anus, ground bone into
        sand — the one
who knelt when they wished it,
in mid–street if they so desired,
in the vein, in the cut, then cut
        each with her call, called
cayenne to the wounds, licked
their cheeks into violet rags before
        every murder. I, who hurried
        falling down love, birth named
        Skeleton, rose
        with a Cherokee back —
        black spine like a drill and the hole
the drill drills, child
        of a woman whose mother
        said, every bedtime,
I've had a girl-child I don't love —
the third breast, the bedpan, thing
        with one shriveled arm
who won't nest with others
so she won't need them — I am
        a bothered land, an aggregate
vessel of stillborn, lapsed flesh closed to seed.
        I,
        who
        lay down
        and opened
        my legs

to strangers, staring ahead as they
fucked me, singing
            the constancy of noon,
chewing skin into fabulous expensive
wet scarves. I am their beautiful rage,
                        awkward
            as a poisoned liver, as
the glut of fear, whose dream is of
            phosphorous deep shining deep
            under the sea, a blue boy's
face pressing the surface of the shallowest
pool of the morning, of the breaking,
            a detail of fine lace
            at his throat, I am
the thin girl child who craves
            his mouth, his tongue,
            his larynx and lung
            as he tells her everything,
            tells her where to go, tells her

            how to get there.

Terminal

I'm waiting for you
       to come home —
         not now or ever.
Listening for the car or door —
         not here, not ever again.
The fountain thickens with algae.
Then driving the highway all night,
         the assault again.
(To the cat:) "We'll need
         each other now sweet one."
It's clear to the left,
       you can go on a little.
This is gonna get really bad.
Come back, not again—as in ever.
         No opening gate, no acoustics.
         Okay, you broke me
so altogether, all that's left
is this lust for sleep.

Such a Widening: Landscape

Between each rib
the September light

comes in much too brightly.
And winter is arriving

with its awful call
to visit personally each

of my faces. I thought
I was done with all this.

Who cares who is born
or who makes bright

for a time the coming dark?
My black hair.

My blackened veins.

Watershed

There are white arms

amidst the smudge

of branches. It's difficult
to speak, to say

there is something terrible in me —

hidden. The last note of a bell.

Beneath my feet the silk weeds,
soaked with dew and frost.

I walk among them.

Beyond the world—dusk.

The body's talent for sorrow
must shine like sapphires.

Perhaps I can't even try anymore,
or won't.

Look up.
Ashes in the air.

Nocturne of Scars

This half moon will pass
and I see wisdom in that.

Not reassurance of waking
but the waking to stillness

under frozen ground.
Not resurrection,

but fists full of cold gladiolas, and
the end of dreams.

If your beloved dies at least you're left loved.
Around me — the flawed city, a cup of ether

one drinks with white lips.
I've tried to close the windows and doors,

but this moon scores letters
all over my skin,

and silence answers emptiness
in vague parables like:

perhaps you believed in love
much more than you really knew.

Carving

Slumber and the harmony of secret scents, rose,
all body damp, and woven by

the patterns of movement between us.
Shaped by twin hours, only our joining could smell that way,

thick with the debts we owed one another.
Your eyelids told tales of dreaming —

perhaps of some young bride's ankles.
Perhaps of ornately sculpted oaken doors

unlatched and slightly ajar.
And when sleep was completely forgotten,

you stood in the kitchen, carefully
describing two old English chisels

you'd just acquired to shape difficult wood.
You said they were the best you'd ever use.

Dream of the Petrified Forest

The root of the human is the voice
and a man sings himself into the world.

And like any ritual beginning,
the lungs, the limbs, twist as in birth or as in death.

This was always the curse of the speaking mouth,
with all the lies and truths carved

from the sting of each sound that brings us

belly to belly with love and love's gasping canyons.

In other words, I took your kiss and so
will choke

in that room behind the eyes
where pain corrects us like an axe.

Oh, yes, it's *always* better to feel hate than nothing,

because time migrates like muscle lost, like smoke.

Wishing is the country of my new home —

land where the sky cascades
and the voice comes from light, from asps

and carbon—thief of yellow.

This from a distance —

the pearled, nearly naked man: blunted, raised

naked man,

the crack of dying things, and
sometimes just knowing someone remembers you

is enough.

Three

Two Kinds of Falling

The first eight of our twenty–foot banana trees fell
late Christmas day 2002. We sat naked by the fire,
drinking hot El Patron from gray green shot glasses
you'd bought in Southern France.
The family had gone, leaving good crystal
and soiled napkins strewn about the laden table,
flames flaring violets and indigo blues while
the Christmas tree lit up in staid heartbeats
of bright bulbs, red satin ribbons, and my grandmother's
transparent glass birds. Warm and flush and drunk
by then, we sat in our skins like old blankets —
well–used and wrapped, and softly easy to touch.

I remember we kissed with agave–oiled lips
before drinking another shot (or two)
and still nude, walking, tentative at first,
then certainly into the slanted silver rain.
I took the small machete. You always used the bigger steel one.
We chopped huge cylinder celery stalks of red–veined
trunks into manageable chunks, slipping, stumbling
through mud–splattering soil and muck until
we were newly brown, until the trees were gone
and we stood near a heap of mulch, our bodies
coated in the deep aroma of fallen
fruit, the wings of dusk settling over us,
a slight green pique to the air as it filtered
the final swirling shards of fronds.

The last two of our twenty–foot trees
toppled tonight through the high black of mid–October
as another plague of rain rained over the city like sin.
And while I watched late night TV, the king of the trees
came to ground with what I knew to be its falling sound,
throwing down along the blue gravel path, and sparing
my delicate garden. In my nightgown, with bare feet,
I addressed the wounded darkness with a huge
flashlight and the small rusted knife still good enough to hack

and slice through the black night, the unforeseen split.
And you, gone for good to the east, to the pines
and the snow's wide white empty canvas.
Mario, the gardener, gave me his home number just
before this heavy rain. Because he knows I'm alone now.
Because he knows those trees have shallow roots,
are top heavy so might just fall easily with the sudden onset
of an unexpected storm.

Ghost

It's finally been determined —
he's becoming *ghost*. Ghost

of chin and brow, of five familiar
footsteps from the kitchen to the door.

Ghost of the green sweater left
on the bed, of the worn blue tee,

work-boots thrown near the hall,
the shared reading glasses;

she bows to each object,
recalls each absent thing.

Close as a fox in a den, turning
again, then again, she nuzzles

the ghosts of his Spanish soap,
old Irish songs, sawdust footprints,

his private clues and whistles,
lost somewhere in the wires. She hears

the thread of his tenor, his tune, of the closing
gray gate, the hot showers lull — as the dinner table

seems sawn in two & Buffy the Vampire
Slayer speaks, muted on TV, miming a lesson

in "aloneness at night," specific concerns, like
naming her own newborn ghost—the pale

waxy mask pooled in his red coffee cup
the one on the counter she still refuses even to touch.

Question

And what will it be
to walk through the 4th
alone, then find the stone
under the bench outside
Musée d'Orsay, and the note
I wrote, then buried there,
for a future him to read?

While he brushed salt
and bits of eggshells from
my lap. While I talked of planting
roses. As a man in a park
threw a green ball to his son.
Before we continued
up the Seine. And an old woman
sat where we'd just been
before our body heat had gone.

There will be no other years.
I will sleep on the floor
in a quiet belonging
to me which won't lie.
He will follow the tree line,
leaving his thumbprints behind
on my throat, to catch the last
pulse as I ask him aloud why
a man would leave the only
things he's ever really loved.

Dream of the Unused Church

This is all I can remember —

light flashes from the eyeglasses of those
lining the high balcony — an eve of strange small birds.

A dwarf baritone who has no arms, yet has both hands,
is singing Mahler's *Kindertotenlieder.*

The thin bald black–clad conductor worships the silence
between movements, fearless of

transition's loss, nearly cruel as he extends
it toward the holy. I sink as if under drifted snow,

which gathers in my eyes and hollows
of my collar bones, and when I've grown robin's-egg blue,

dread rushes up from the edges of the woods

where Mahler pens for perpetuity his mourning.

With each widening ring of silence
huge trees begin to freeze

as you, ahead in the distance, stumble
off the steps of the white church where

I've always seen us dancing through
swirling orchards of blue snow.

And so I realize I have failed, am alone before
the quiet wooden house, each unlit window

reflecting naked frozen birch and beech,
small dead birds gleaming like well–cut diamonds.

Not even a crow ruffles this pastoral,
the quiet, the first inch of death.

I raise my eyes to a hall of nodding white heads —
Kabuki masks, a hive of people

simply falling asleep or into the deep spell of melancholy —

and know that in the genius of eternity,
we're imperceptible as air.

Still, night is fully tangible, so perhaps this
is my actual death. Really, how would I ever know?

Perhaps if I'm quiet, we'll travel again by sleigh
into the naked birch, the beech, perhaps the music —

Across the Canyon

What do you see, dear heart,

through the distance —
indictment, memory over fact,

the dead stare of aftermath?

An unexpected hurricane

    and dusk fills
with perfect sparrows flying

hard through thunder.

Many have lied to themselves
    before. Who can say

    who is

    deserving?

A difficult birth left her body
weightless with pain,

almost invisible.

The bells are ringing.
The bells are

    ringing, ringing.

Nightfall, Wattle's Mansion, June 14, 1986

Behind us, across the long expanse of lawn
our guests blow ten thousand bubbles
instead of throwing rice. They crowd, all dressed
up like paper cut-out dolls, under the 1940s noir arches.

My grandmother, who, due to turbulence, vomited
all the way from Milwaukee, witnessed the marriage papers
with her spidery hand. It's the last time I will see her alive.
She leans against your mother, who, wearing her

famous lavender gown, stands right beside your
brother in his gold oval rims. He has just met
my own brother. They will become friends.
They've told me there's no film left in any of the cameras,

nothing to catch this momentary waterfall
of bubbles drifting out towards the downtown city lights.
Silver blossoms that float like promises
over our heads where with each step in the newly wet grass

my satin heels sink deep, stick, then release.
And the damp wing of my veil rises into wind.
And I whisper, "Remember this. Remember.
Because it's all we'll have of it, forever."

Highway 99

You downshift into the yam heat.
In the valley of grapevines
we don't talk of childlessness.
Your elbow is a wing in the open window
as a confetti of leaves and shadows
rush by. I know you've never seen
these orchards in spring bloom —
how the pink lanterns of light float down.
Red potatoes lie on the ground now,
the color of dried blood.
I make the sign of the cross.
The King's River smells of drowned cattle.
Then Exitor, Pixley, *terra bonita*, sweet dirt
all around as faithful to the sky
as water is to gravity. In Delano, sweethearts
will wait past midnight, when heat
carries them to each other.
Your left shoulder is burning
with the setting sun. I sleep and dream
there is a family by the roadside
dressed in Easter clothes. *Abuela. Mama.*
The *padre's* good Panama hat points brim down
under the car's yawning hood
as the smallest girl's red dress
opens like a tulip. She holds a grace
of white blossoms, loco weed,
bridal bouquet. I reach for her.
I reach for you. In a swarm,
battling ants cross and re-cross
her two best shoes. Behind her,
sunflowers snake through the barbed wire.
I give you a palm full of almond blossoms.
I dream of tumbleweeds, divining rods
and soil. When I wake it isn't Easter after all.
Still we have to go to church
take what we can harvest.

Dream of Carrying

There is a man. He is brown.
He is white, then brown again,
cut from the shifting
shadow cast off from deep snow banking over
the austere, untamed country
through which we ride.
The car is huge inside and outside
it's the silver of a sky named
after a king who died in a bygone era
so long ago it can barely be remembered.
I am not me, yet am myself.
I hold a child who is brown,
then black, then simply one little one
sleeping over my left shoulder, the collar
bones of which are sharp, on which she suckles,
her breath a mink cowl rounding my neck
as she murmurs a baby's desires, all soft,
and still closely tinted with ash.
Her bones are mice,
shells whistling with stars and souls.
She is mine and has been saved.
The man's name is Sadness or Valor, his
religion — a barter with each mournful
measure of time, the sequences
of a past he has surrendered
yet still carries in his constant gaze.
We face ahead, sense the grasping night —
the only one we'll ever have. It is beautiful
in the seeded distance, a horizon of spiraling trees
waiting in unborn grace, each curve
submitting to snow–light, as transient
yet as steady as his enormous
hand, the brown, white cloven hoof
covering mine over the gear shift.
Shifting into the cave of my breasts, she coughs
once but does not wake. And we
wonder — will she? Ever?

Mountain

Then rain
obscures my hands,
before the glance
of white sun, when
for one moment,
I can let go —
see what we are.
Forgive me.

New Year: Day

I remember winter
as cold
and cold and eating in silence

   and waiting in blue.

And what does one do with want?

Here are the things I take
   as my lovers now —

this room spread with amber lights of flame —
this, my chair, equals peace —

that old Persian rug —
the old love story
of one weaver and his threads.

I have been studying
the severed parts of a mammal's heart,

the low candle wicking

as I marked each pewter vein in a book.
I spent the first hours

   diving into the blue

acres of molten lavender — clouds
collapsing, the cries
of odd birds, prehistoric

and slated with memories, each one
   which, of course, must include a goodbye.

It was a first-rate study of rainbows, all colors
in bands, both surgery and satiation,

open to the core,
the new indebted to the old,

the first hours spent
without the dead spell of the past.

I lost a love.
But I did not lose

love.

Dissolve: A Coda

You slowly untangle your hair

as the gardenias sink into the bowl.

Then your breath over the black circle of tea
in a stained white cup.

How the yellowed gloves you found still fit
after years in a drawer.

How you meet a shuffling woman in
an empty street, as wind tests each threshold and doorknob.

And hours later, following the waves

back the way you came, you'll watch a
surprised man catch fish after silver fish,

the always, then indigo mountains,
north, and continually changing.

Acknowledgments

The following poems have appeared previously in these publications:

The Yalobusha Review: "Morning"

The Cider Press Review: "Nightfall, Wattle's Mansion, June 14, 1986"; "San Miguel"

Pool: "Highway 99"

Art Life: "Dream of the Blue Woman"; "Dream of Carrying"; "Dream of the Petrified Forest"

River Styx: "Patterns of Migration"

Mental Shoes: "Quiet. Blue. Murder."; "Dream, Untitled"; "Mountain"

Askew: "Outside the Church of the Freedom Fighters"

I extend deep gratitude to my teachers David St. John, Ralph Angel, Cecelia Woloch, and to The Monday Night Poetry Posse (Sarah Maclay, Jim Natal, Jan Wesley, Marjorie Becker, Brenda Yates, Paul Lieber, Jeanette Clough, and Dina Hardy) for their ongoing, rigorous and close attention to the work.

Notes

The epigraph "Mort" is a definition taken from *The American Heritage Dictionary,* Third Edition, copyright 1992.

Farewell to Spring: California wildflowers whose blooming signals the arrival of summer and splatters the newly brown hills with lavender during a short transitional interval.

The Petrified Forest is a US national park located in Arizona State. The "trees" in question are fossilized logs washed there in floods 200-250 million years ago. They consist mainly of *Araucarioxylon arizonicum.* Two others, *Woodworthia* and *Schilderia,* occur in small quantities in the north end of the park. All three are now extinct.

San Miguel refers to San Miguel de Allende, one of Mexico's colonial cities located in nearly the geographic center of the country and settled in 1542.

Regarding "The Church of the Freedom Fighters": San Miguel de Allende's namesake was independence leader Ignacio Allende. The church in question was once his home.

Churros: a common Mexican oblong bread rolled in sugar, frequently spiced with cinnamon and sold by street vendors and pastry shops.

The Kilauea volcano, on the Island of Hawaii, is one of earth's most active. Said to be home to Pele, the volcano goddess of ancient Hawaiian legends, it's also the namesake of the nearby famous surfing beach.

Agave: the cactus from whence both tequila and mescal come; is grown primarily in northern Mexico.

Buffy the Vampire Slayer: Twenty-first-century purveyor of wisdom and entertainment.

The 4th in "Question" refers to the fourth arrondissement or the Marais in Paris.

Wattle's Mansion: located behind the community garden at Franklin Boulevard just above Hollywood Boulevard in Hollywood, California.

Highway 99: one of two main interstate highways running north and south through California's central farmlands.

The line in "Flight," *your absence is a presence,* owes an acknowledgement to Wilfred Bion (1897-1979), the British psychoanalyst who spoke of the absence of the mother as the presence (or etiology) of another sort of psychic experience.

The images, and perhaps too, something of the quiet nature of birches and beeches in "Dream of the Unused Church" owe a debt to David St. John's two poems, "Beeches," and "The Red Leaves of Night," from his book, *The Red Leaves of Night.*

Author Biography

Holiday Mason, a resident of Venice, CA, graduated from Antioch University with a bachelor's degree in liberal arts and a master's degree in clinical psychology. She is currently a therapist in private practice. New Rivers Press published her first book of poetry, *Towards the Forest,* in 2007. Her second book, *Dissolve,* was a finalist for the 2005 Autumn House Press Prize and a semi-finalist for both The Backwater Press and The Tupelo Press awards. She has authored two chapbooks, *Light Spilling From Its Own Cup* (Inevitable Press, 1999) and *Interlude* (Far Star Fire Press, 2001). Her poems have appeared in numerous publications including *Poetry International* and *American Literary Review*. Mason has served as artist-in-residence for the Beyond Baroque Literary Arts Center, for which she co-edited the anthology *Echo 681*.